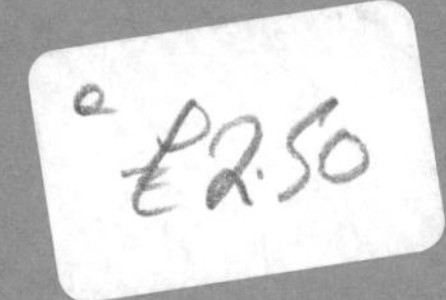

£2.50

AF477091

MURDER ME

MURDERME

Joanna Kirk

Published in 2009 by
Murderme
14 Welbeck Street
London
W1G 9XU

Designed by
Emma Scott-Child

Photography of artworks by
Prudence Cuming Associates

Copyediting and coordination by
Kate Davies

Joanna Kirk would like to thank
Peter, Clara and Anders

Distributed by
Other Criteria
www.othercriteria.com

Standard edition: ISBN 978-1-906957-08-7
Signed edition: ISBN 978-1-906957-09-4

Joanna
Kirk

Morning Song

Love set you going like a fat gold watch.
The midwife slapped your footsoles, and your bald cry
Took its place among the elements.

Our voices echo, magnifying your arrival. New statue.
In a drafty museum, your nakedness
Shadows our safety. We stand round blankly as walls.

I'm no more your mother
Than the cloud that distills a mirror to reflect its own slow
Effacement at the wind's hand.

All night your moth-breath
Flickers among the flat pink roses. I wake to listen:
A far sea moves in my ear.

One cry, and I stumble from bed, cow-heavy and floral
In my Victorian nightgown.
Your mouth opens clean as a cat's. The window square

Whitens and swallows its dull stars. And now you try
Your handful of notes;
The clear vowels rise like balloons.

Sylvia Plath. 19 February 1961

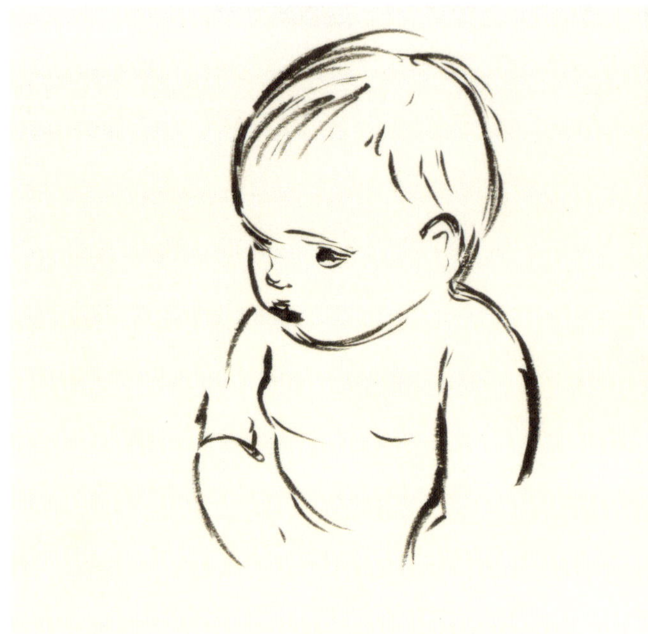

Untitled sketch, 2003
Joanna Kirk

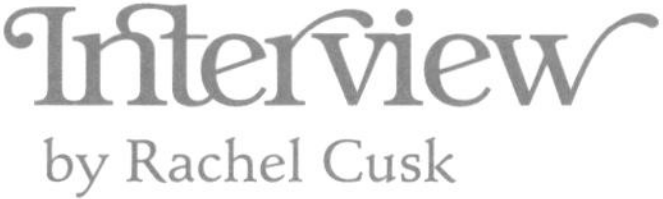

Interview

by Rachel Cusk

RC. I wanted to start by asking about your materials.

JK. Well, I've used pastel for years and years. I love using it. The history of pastel is quite interesting because there are very few great artists who used pastel, apart from people like Degas and Odilon Redon and Mary Cassatt. It always seemed to me to be a very delicate medium. And even though the work has a delicacy about it, it's just pure pigment. I'm also just using my fingers; there's not a paintbrush in the way. So the surface, to me, with my images, with my pictures, is really important and vital. It's almost like delicately putting something on and then building something up quite gradually layer by layer. There's a kind of hardness to it and also a softness in the actual material.

RC. Have you arrived at that pastel process through some kind of journey?

JK. I never liked painting. When I started at college they said "Oh you need to try painting, Jo. You're drawing all the time." Then one tutor came along and said "Actually, no, it's fine, do drawings, you don't need to do painting." And so I found a way of using colour by using pastels. It's just something I love. I love pastel sticks. I love breaking them. It's a real pleasure just going and seeing them in trays and buying the pastels – these lovely colours – and using a beautiful surface and building the surface up. It takes a long time. I mean Paula Rego uses pastels but I think there aren't many who use them and can use them quite well. It's just something I've really developed, and I can't see myself using any other medium.

RC. Do you still sketch?

JK. I do sketch. I use pens and pencils. But my main medium is pastel painting. In a way, they're not drawings. These are pastel paintings.

RC. What's the relationship between drawing and painting, and where does pastel come in that, on that graph?

JK. Well, I think drawing is always seen as something that's more immediate in a way. If you're sketching you're putting down a drawing quite quickly.

RC. But is it also more honest or truthful?

JK. There is something about that. People always want to look at artists' drawings, don't they? They want to see behind the scenes and look at an artist's drawing to see where you're coming from. And, in fact, I don't ever do sketches of these big pieces. But I've always drawn. Ever since I was tiny I have drawn. My mother always said to me that until I started drawing I had a really bad temper. It was frustration. I had to control everything. I had my pushchair, walking along with dolls in it, and every time, she said, we'd have to stop and sort the dolls out before we carried on with our walk. And then I started drawing and she said it was like therapy, which I don't know if it's true so much. I don't want to say it's therapy because it isn't. It's much more than that.

RC. So that story of you as a child brings me to the subject of your evolution as an artist, and whether you can just say a bit about it.

JK. Years ago I did two huge portraits of my parents, massive portraits. I've always been drawing or drawn to something that's not necessarily family-orientated but something that's close to me or near me – friends, family. Years ago I did a whole series of portraits of my friends smiling. And that was quite an image because they were great, blown-up pictures of my girlfriends, all just laughing and smiling. It was a very confrontational piece because it wasn't smiling in a nice way. It was really acting. It was very threatening and quite horrific in some ways, not this gentle, loving thing. There was no attempt to flatter anybody in it. Then I was working as a receptionist at a law firm and hated the job so much I got people who worked there to make these little things out of plasticine. I gave them a packet of children's plasticine each and said "Make something". So all these people were doing little plasticine sculptures. I photographed them, blew them up, did these huge drawings of them, with all the little indentations where fingers had been. So they were child-like yet from adults in this very corporate world making effigies of things. The title of each piece was the name of the person who had made the effigy. They were extraordinary. That was my way of dealing with my situation. I was sitting at reception reading *American*

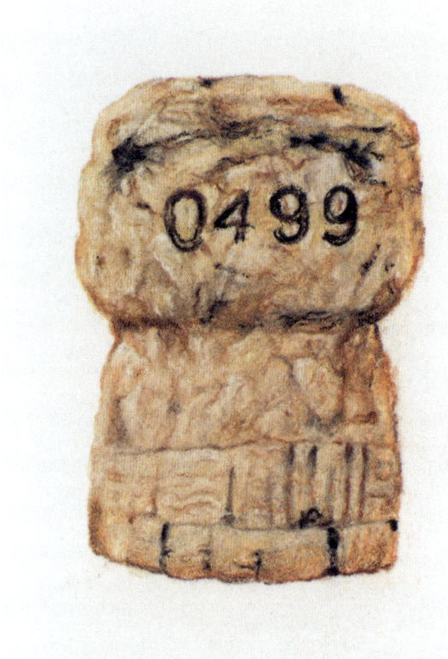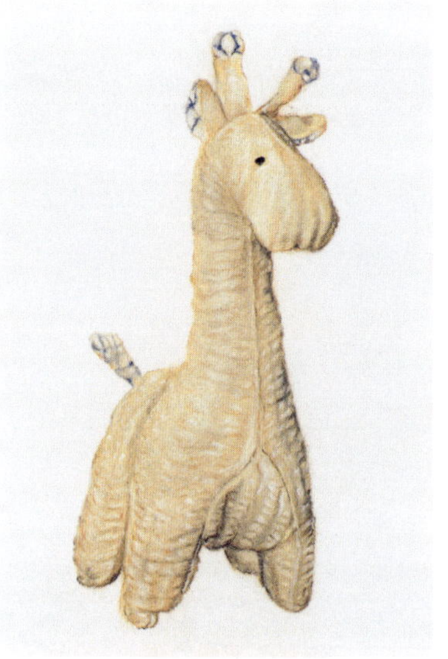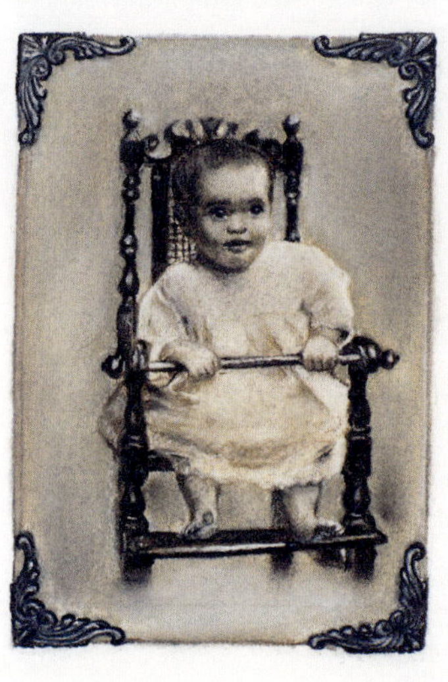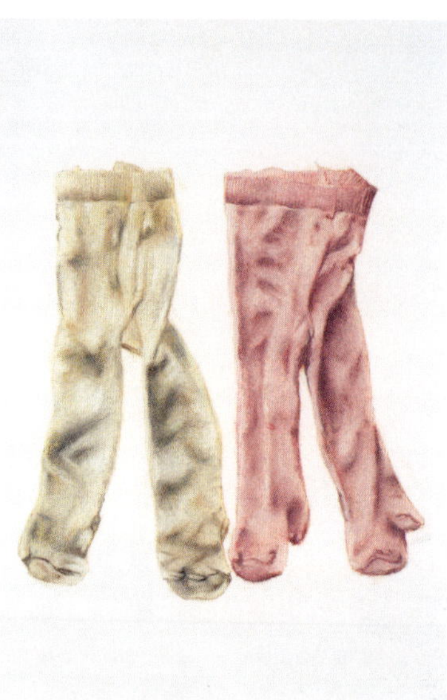

Psycho by Bret Easton Ellis [laughs] trying to cope with my surroundings and wanting desperately to get on with my art work.

RC. So do you think people are innately artists? There's a whole therapy based around getting people to do this stuff, the idea being that adults have to be taught again how to play.

JK. When these little things came back you'd just see that they were very lovingly made. It was probably a very subversive thing to do.

RC. This is something I see in writing as well: that all children can write stories and all children can write poems, and by the time they become young adults they can't do it any more, and by the time they are middle-aged they want to come and do a creative writing course.

JK. Absolutely. But then I went on to doing a large piece about my husband, Peter, called *All in a Day*, which is tiny images of me and Peter. It was just about spending a day together and the ritual of spending a day together. The images are of our heads only, without the bodies, without seeing what was really going on. In a way quite Catholic. A small celebration – quite ritualistic and almost fetishising the relationship in a way with a drink and food, a bath. But just very gentle. Not a huge kind of "Hey, this is us!" But this is our life. After that I did a piece when I was pregnant of me standing in my studio, completely naked with sock marks. This was exhibited along with *All in a Day*. It's not the most flattering of pictures – I wouldn't want to show it now. I'm standing

there in my studio, and there are all sorts of scuff marks, it's really grotty looking, but with some lipstick on, but naked. And it's not even a full pregnancy but that sort of in-between stage. You don't know what you are. You just feel fat and weird. And I was thinking "Where am I? I'm going to have a baby. It's obvious in a way. This is my creative life and where am I going to go now and what's going to happen to me? This is where I am."

RC. I wanted to talk about that. These pictures are obviously about children and, to me, in my experience – my artistic experience – being able to create around children implies not a break with the past exactly but a caesura of some sort. And I just wondered whether that meant anything to you?

JK. When I was pregnant I read this amazing book called *Collecting Souls, Gathering Dust* about Alice Neel and Rhoda Medary, which in fact another artist had lent me.[1] It's about these two women's lives as artists and mothers. Alice Neel kept making her work regardless of the difficulties in her life. She had a really tough life. She didn't have any money. I don't remember how many children she had. She was bringing them up on her own, living in a really small room, really hanging on to her painting. That's what comes across in the book anyway. And then the other woman, Rhoda Medary, got married, abandoned her talents, always kept meaning to paint, but didn't have Alice Neel's drive. At the end of the book, Alice Neel had kept working and become successful. It had remained central to her life. And Rhoda Medary, though she eventually

[1] Gerald and Margaret Belcher, *Collecting Souls, Gathering Dust: The Struggles of Two American Artists* (Paragon House, New York, 1991)

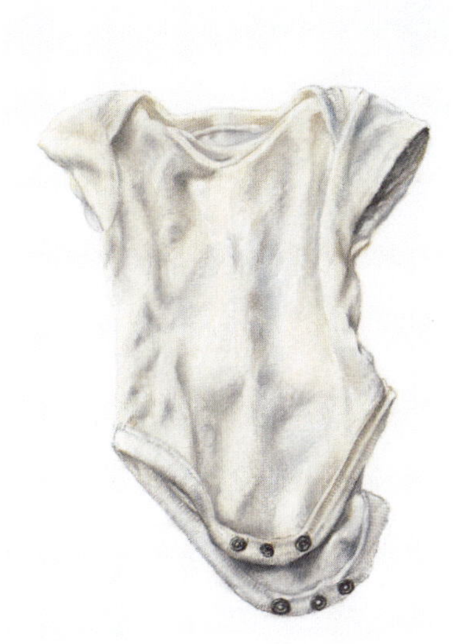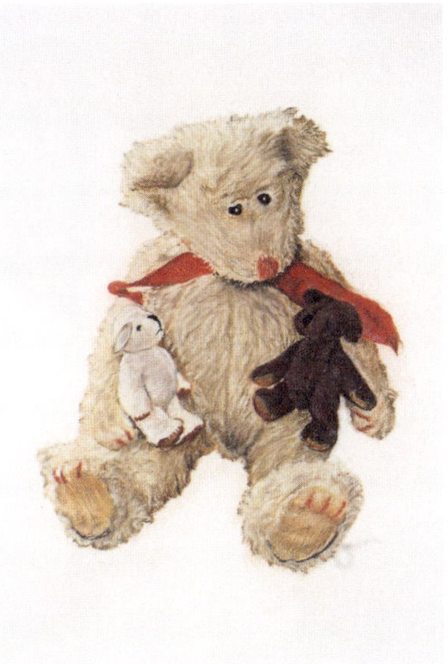

It's A Girl, 2000
Joanna Kirk

had an exhibition…well, it hadn't been central to her life. Other things had got in the way. It said it all to me. I was terrified, actually, of becoming a person who didn't make art. Terrified. And I didn't think it was going to happen to me but there is always at the back of your mind that fear of giving up on something, of giving up on being true to yourself when you have children. You as a writer talk about this idea of leaving yourself. You talked about the mother, the 'motherbaby', and that concept of being joined together. Your identity is so wrapped up in that child. Once I remember going to town on the train after I'd had my first child, Clara. It reminded me of the piece in your book *A Life's Work* when you were in Oxford Street and it was completely shocking for you to be alone. You saw that woman trying on clothes with the child and you said "Go home, you've got to go home".

RC. Which I never did.

JK. No, I didn't either. But I saw people with babies and I wanted to have a badge to say, "I've got a child as well," even though I was having time on my own and knew I had to get some time on my own so I could find my own way again. But it's a huge thing that happens because the change is phenomenal.

RC. For me, motherhood was where I found the severed thread of writing. And clearly it did have to be found somewhere in the children because it was chaos outside my world with them. My single identity – I didn't really know what that was. The writer's identity that I'd

always had – I didn't know what had become of that. So the creativity had to be found through the children. I just wonder if that's something you experienced?

JK. Yes, absolutely. I had my daughter Clara, and about three months after she was born, no sooner than that, I did a piece called *It's a Girl* – tiny little drawings about her, very sweet, very precise drawings. Her fist, for example, my breast with milk coming out, cards, little toys and babygros, a nappy, because one's inspecting their nappies the whole time – all that obsessive interest in the children. So I made that into something for myself as well. I wanted to make my experience of her, this person coming into the world, which everybody experiences. It's a cliché but a lot of people have this happening. But I wanted to make something that, even though it was such a normal thing for me, was really quite extraordinary – all these tiny things that are in your home, to do with her, little gifts. I did a tiny drawing of Peter's mother when she was a child, this very connected family portrait of her having just been born. And then I used to find myself going for walks all the time in the park. The park was just a godsend for me. So then I did a piece called *Moth-Breath* – a phrase from a Sylvia Plath poem called 'Morning Song' – which consisted of portraits of my daughter's head and then next to that would be something in the park, like the light falling on the bench or a squirrel, a worm or a nut. So it's odd, quite sinister – an antithesis of a Richard Long walk. You know, he goes for these big walks…

RC. Yes.

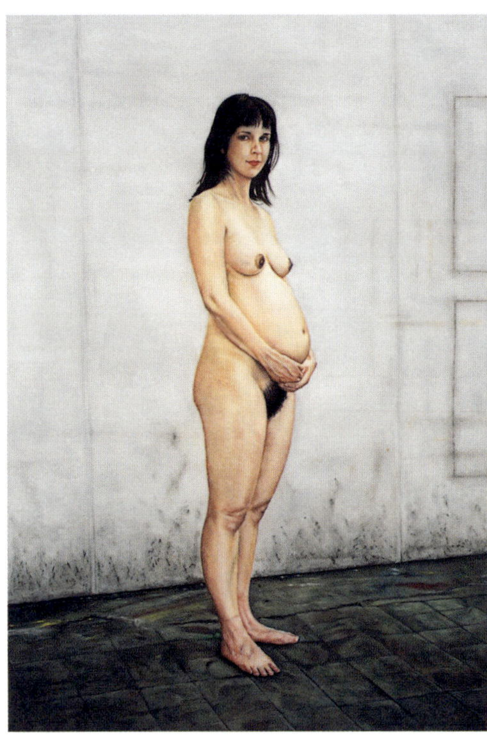

Conceptual, 1999
Joanna Kirk

JK. But mine was with a baby. And I was starting to think of nature as well.
But always using the children in the work because that was the only way
I could find a means of dealing with the change in my life. I also couldn't
understand why the hell no one else was making work about being a
mother, unless it was bloody, literally gory. There's either that side of it
with art or the very sentimental side. I remember going to Tate Modern,
trying to find a piece of art that I could relate to, and I found a Mary Kelly
piece, *Analysed Markings And Diary Perspective Schema (Experimentum Mentis
III: Weaning from the Dyad)*, which she did in 1975 as part of her 'Post-Partum
Document'. It was very conceptual, but it was all about her child starting
nursery and, to me, it was like diagrams interspersed with how she felt
about him starting nursery and his birth. It was an academic piece but it
wasn't even quite that. It seemed relevant to me, which was why I also
loved your book *A Life's Work*, because I was trying to find something and
I was thinking "Well, look, this book, she's obviously doing this – living
her life and describing what is actually happening and yet making it
universal." And I always felt that was what I wanted to do. I think it's
incredible that there aren't millions of books being written about this or
millions of art pieces. I don't know why it is that people don't feel that they
can write or make work about this experience.

RC. Well, there are two things: one is that it's very difficult to create
something when you've created children; the other is that there is
a snobbery about the whole endeavour of representing motherhood.
Men are allowed to do it: it's fine for the great American males to write
domestic novels. It's almost as though a man dignifies that sphere by his

artistic presence in it, whereas a woman has merely failed to get out and
see the world.

JK. I think perhaps that's true of the art world as well.

RC. I wonder whether this is a particular difficulty in the visual arts:
locating what femaleness is. In literature, femaleness can wax and wane
in terms of how much power a woman writer feels she has at any given
moment in her society. But that process of articulation of otherness,
which is what I think female literature is, began, in the novel anyway,
with Charlotte Brontë and Jane Austen. So an English woman novelist
feels a sense of having forebears, of having intellectual parents, some sort
of past. And I just wondered whether there is that sense of the past for a
female artist?

JK. To a degree. Mary Cassatt was an Impressionist who isn't celebrated
in the same way as Degas, and her work was about mothers and children,
and they're wonderful, stunning pieces. Yet she just didn't get the acclaim
of Degas. Berthe Morisot is another one. There's a beautiful painting
of hers called *The Cradle*, where she's looking into a little cot and there's
a veil over the baby. I love that painting. It's a really gentle image, but
powerful.

RC. Another reason for the scarcity of female representations of
domesticity may be that a lot of female artists don't have children.
Motherhood exists in direct competition with your work and, very

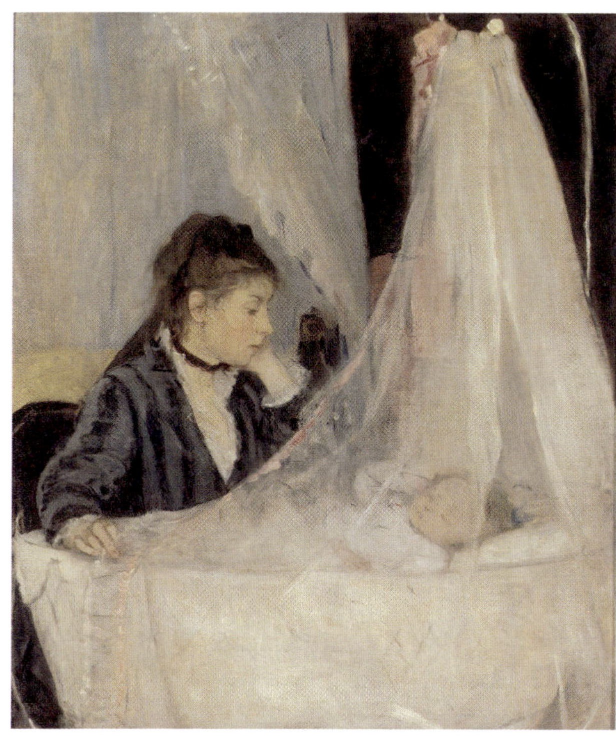

Le Berceau (The Cradle), 1872
Berthe Morisot

sensibly, you might say, there are women artists who choose not to fight that battle because it's possible that you'll lose it.

JK. Absolutely. It's interesting. Mary Kelly is an artist who was also a tutor at Goldsmith's College in London, where I went. She used to come into college to have conversations, although I didn't really have any conversations with her at the time. She was extremely intellectual to me then. I didn't have a clue what she was on about. In hindsight, I realise how fantastic she is. She did the 'Post-Partum Document' piece I mentioned earlier, in which she put her child's nappies up at the Institute of Contemporary Arts in London. And she documented exactly what was happening…I mean this is incredible work because it was so brave. There was actually a furore about it. It was messy art.

RC. But in a way you've put your finger on the difficulty – and I've had this accusation levelled at me too: that you can seem exploitative as a woman artist. That accusation is bandied about very, very easily: putting your child's dirty nappies up on the wall; taking photographs of your children and exhibiting them; or indeed writing intimately about your children and allowing complete strangers to read it.

JK. But you can be objective about it. You don't have to be totally confessional, although you do have to relinquish something in yourself. I mean, I'm not interested in being confessional about my life. My work is not about my relationship with my children. It doesn't go into that kind of area.

RC. So, just talking about the paintings themselves, on the subject of children, I admit that I've read various things into these images. One of the most striking things about them is the evocation of something very, very, particular that I feel about children – that happens around children – which is the intense relationship between the subjective and the objective. And that, in a way, is what a relationship with a child is. It seems to me partly what these paintings are about. So the child is both subject and object, and lost in the landscape at the same time as seeming to create the landscape. So it's almost like the two things at the same time: that the landscape seems to be stemming from them but it's also enclosing them in this incredibly complicated way.

JK. Yes.

RC. As we were saying earlier, they're obviously being looked at because their mother or father isn't in the picture, so that immediately implies that the parent is the one perceiving them. It's very much a parent's perception of the child, but the landscape is almost like their own – the child's own imaginative projection. Which leads me to my question, which is: are you saying that the child is to be envied for its freedom and its power of imagination?

JK. Yes, I think it's definitely that. They are in their own worlds and very isolated in those worlds. There's not – apart from the pushchair with my handbag – myself in them. And there's a sense of abandonment about them. That's another thing with having children, which you have written about it in *A Life's Work*: this sense of them being on their own. And, also, the thing you have as a parent is the complete and utter worry of them out there in the world without you. The fact that children are always, from the day they're born – well, if you're lucky enough to be a nurtured child – looked at and, not obsessed over, but looked at all the time. Where are you? Are you next door? Are you here in the garden? Watching them. And that continually goes on from the day that they're born. You are constantly observing them. So in the landscapes that I have done, they feel like they're being taken over and they're quite alienating. And in some of the works it feels they could be in a threatening environment. When you were writing *A Life's Work* about parental love, you say:

If parental love is the blueprint for all loves, it is also a re-enactment, a vision, and investigation of self-love. When I care for my daughter I revisit my own vulnerability, my primordial helplessness. I witness that which I cannot personally remember, my early existence in this white state, this world of milk and shadows and nothingness. My survival testifies to the fact that I, too, was cared for, and yet again and again I experience images of abandonment, of lack of love, unable to stop myself from pursuing ghoulish narratives of what would happen if I left her. If I went out for the day. If I failed to pick her up when she cried or refused to feed her. Having lived for so long high up in the bickering romantic quarters of love, it is as if I were suddenly cast down to its basement, its foundations. Love is more respectful, more practical, more hardworking than I had ever suspected, but it lies close to the power to destroy.[2]

And I think that's really interesting – the love, the feeling of love.

RC. But that's ambivalence though, isn't it? The imagining of some harm coming to your child is ambivalence – that unconsciously, you are the one who wants to bring this harm to your child and so you re-imagine it as some danger that they're in from the world.

JK. In a way, I thought of doing paintings with my children hanging off precipices and stuff, which I'd have to do with Photoshop, which I don't want to use. [laughs] I have thought about going to the Arctic and sort of putting them on a bit of ice. That would be a great picture. Yes, they are in worlds that are possibly threatening, and decaying, dying worlds as well. A lot of them are dead leaves and dead trees, so there are obviously references to mortality. And, yes, there is a feeling of them being out there alone in the world and me watching them and...but it's not just that either...it's me out there as well.

RC. So the other thing I wondered, just on this same subject, is the striking fact of how much sort of infinity there is in the detail that's around the children. You've chosen landscapes in which you're going to have to do amazingly detailed and repetitive work. And so what I

wondered was whether this was a representation of servitude – this artistic labour around a very free, carefree child? It's almost as if you're subjected by this work, this duty to fill in around them. You've chosen to enslave yourself in a way, to that detail.

JK. Every area of the piece has to be rendered and looked at. So there is not one area that is more important than the other. It's almost like honouring something. The more I put into it, the more you're going to have to look at it. You can't just walk away from it. From a distance I want people to look at the pieces and think "My God, what the heck is going on here?" I want it to be controlled chaos in other words.

RC. But is it in some way a symbol of the work of being a mother?

JK. Yes. Laborious.

RC. There's this child, singing and dancing.

JK. Yes, especially in *Slate*. It's interesting because, also, it's a mine and people died in that place. And I was completely aware of this. It wasn't just a nice slate mine with lots of bits of rock. It was also a really harsh, manufactured, man-made landscape as well, which is unusual because the others are all completely natural. And I thought...I really wanted her to do a cartwheel – and she had these bright little coloured contemporary clothes on – because I just think it looked great. I didn't want her looking depressed in that landscape, because it is depressing already – very harsh, bleak. You know the history of the slate mines: it's a really hard, extremely male reality, and then you've got this lovely little girl just doing a cartwheel, like "Oh, I'm just going to do a cartwheel". So it's really nice, that thing happening in that landscape.

RC. I see in the new work that you've almost gone further in terms of the relationship of the ratio of the child to the canvas. I mean the size of the canvas as well. The children are getting bigger and so the compass of their world has grown.

JK. Yes, in the new work I just want the landscape to be much more encroaching. They aren't portraits of the children. The pieces are about children active in landscape. And in a new piece I have been working on my daughter is running through the landscape. But it has a Greek feel about it. It is epic, or meant to be epic. She is running through...you're not quite sure whether she's walking or she's running. What is she doing here? I want there to be an element of mystery about the pieces. It feels like there is a narrative attached to each of the pieces...But, yes, they are obviously very carefree children in a very intense and obviously exaggerated landscape as well. There is a lot of history in the rocks and the trees and the leaves. Years and years of overgrowth. What are they? Who are they?

[2] Rachel Cusk, *A Life's Work: On Becoming a Mother* (Fourth Estate, London, 2001), p. 84.

RC. That sense of age, the warping of these various forms and the way forms are created in these landscapes – it's mesmerising. I saw all sorts of funny little faces in the undergrowth. And that crystallised for me into something else, which is that the pictures remind me of the illustrations in the fairy tales that I read as a child. And, more importantly, they remind me of looking at the pictures as a child and of reading as a child, of my experiences of both of those things. And this is particularly true in *Rocks* with the image of your little girl sitting by the waterfall. That's exactly the sort of picture that I would have stared at for such a long time as a child, trying to work out whether it meant something magical or something threatening, and usually it was both. I think, to me, that is what being a child is all about – the mingling of that feeling of mystery and fear with this amazing feeling of magic. Is that a just comparison?

JK. Yes, it is. I loved children's books, particularly Beatrix Potter . I loved her drawings. They seemed sinister…I mean, on the edge. They are dark stories. Beautiful. And her botanical and scientific drawings are fantastic as well. I also loved Arthur Rackham. I think his work is serious. When I was younger, I'd always be drawing trees, fairies and people in woods. Yes, there's definitely an element of magic about it, although I think if I was doing made-up people it would be just fantasy. But there's a reality to my work. And yet there is that magic on top…the way it's rendered and drawn. But, also, because I work with photography, I'm choosing areas that aren't time-sensitive, of a certain time, because it's universal. Like the woods – it could be Hansel and Gretel. But I'm not that interested in fairy tales. I'm not going down a mythical route.

RC. No, it's more just a memory of what it's like being a child, and those early experiences of reading and of looking at pictures are of fairy tales.

JK. I always loved line drawings as well. I loved *Milly Molly Mandy* and E.H. Shepard's illustrations for A.A Milne's books *When We Were Young* and *Now We Are Six*. Those little illustrations with the young boy – very linear, really exquisite drawings.

RC. They're amazingly simple.

JK. Simple, yes, but so beautifully drawn.

RC. Can you tell me more about your influences?

JK. Well, I think your writing, actually [laughs]. I do. I like a lot of Sylvia Plath's poetry. I think she writes about nature and children in quite a shocking way – a really brutal way, but in quite a beautiful way as well. And in painting I like the Impressionists: Berthe Morisot, Degas. Thomas Gainsborough, as well.

RC. Really?

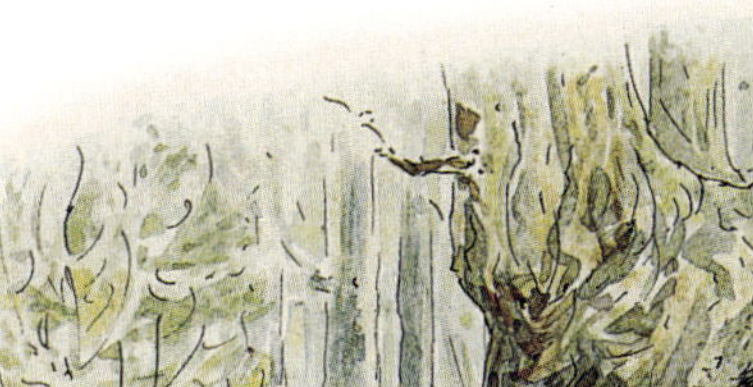

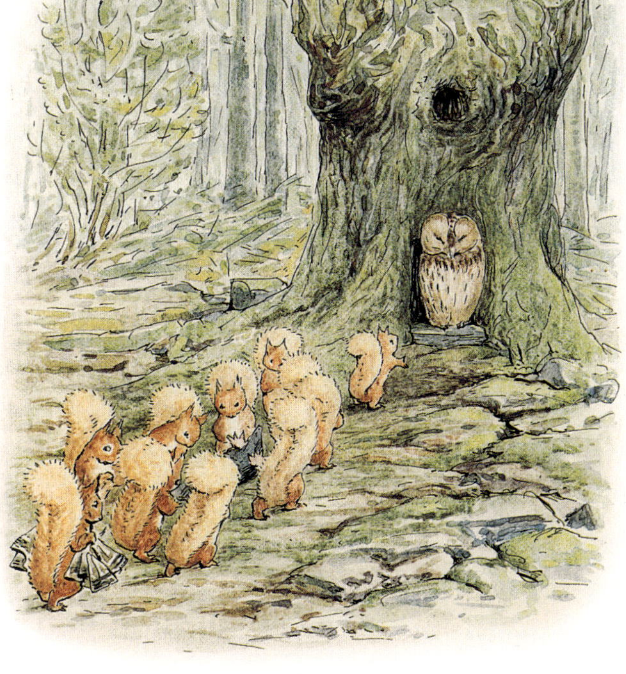

Illustration from *The Tale of Squirrel Nutkin,* 1903
Beatrix Potter

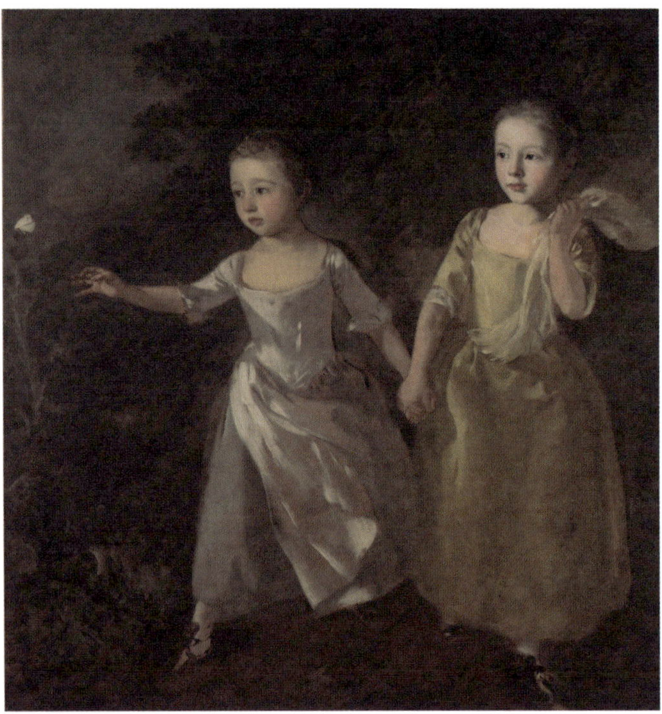

The Painter's Daughters Chasing a Butterfly, c. 1756
Thomas Gainsborough

JK. There is a fantastic portrait he did of his two girls called *The Painter's Daughters Chasing a Butterfly*. The girls grew up to have not terribly happy lives. So it's a bit of a premonition of their little lives. And there's something about the eldest one – they're about four and six years old – she's holding her sister's hand and they're reaching out but they're on this journey in this wood together. And yet you just know, certainly now, what's going to lie ahead in the future of these children. And I think that's the other thing about my work. I'm thinking "They've got the future ahead of them. What are they going to be like? What's it going to be like when they're older? What's going to happen?" There's a feeling lof, not doom, but melancholy, as well. There are no smiling faces.

RC. You very much get the impression of the bigness of the world and the smallness of them.

JK. And, also, our world, which is getting wrecked. You know, nature is in there as well, the feeling of nature continuing, thriving, as well – regardless of us.

RC. Yes… well… and of them belonging to it in the end, or in the beginning.

JK. Käthe Kollwitz I used to like a lot as well because it's very drawing-based. Strong beautiful drawings.

RC. And what about in terms of your contemporaries?

JK. I love Louise Bourgeois. She is, as we speak, in her nineties now. She's just so extreme. She relives the past traumas of her life, all the time, to keep making art. Her work is often huge, very beautiful. She makes rooms or cells with different materials and objects hanging together. It all comes from her childhood. Even though she is an elderly woman now, it's all stemming from her childhood. It's fascinating to me that she's constantly reliving that childhood. She had a solo show at Tate Modern in 2007 that was great. I took my daughter to see it. The first room was full of these drawings of women trapped in houses. They were beautiful drawings – a female body in a house, trapped. And for me it felt like being domestically trapped in a home. And I walked round with my daughter and said "Clara, when you're older you don't need to be trapped in your home all day, cleaning or doing anything like that. You've got to be out there in the world." This sort of says it all in a funny sort of way. It was poignant as well. I really enjoyed going round that show with her.

Annette Messager is another artist whose work I like. Her work seems to be about imagination in childhood – intense but playful sort of pieces.

RC. Do you have any particular relationship to photography, given that you take a lot of photos?

JK. No. I just use it as a device. I don't need a high-tech camera. I'm not interested in the technical. I like to have what I work from in my hand and I like to look at them and think about what I'm going to do with them. So, no, I'm not into messing around with a photograph. It's just a device. And the work, for me, evolves most of all on the paper. Originally my work was photographic but it seems to be moving away from that. They are activated kind of surfaces, so they're about pastel painting as well.

RC. That's interesting because what you say is true and yet the mode of perception is photographic.

JK. Yes. It's real.

RC. And I just wondered whether you perhaps related to photographic artists?

JK. There are great photographers but I like to see a surface. When you are looking at a painting you can keep going back to it, almost freshly each time, you can see something in it. I find with a lot of photography, you look at it once and get the image, and that's fine. But looking at something that's actually manufactured by hand – there is so much that will be going on with the surface. It's a very different experience.

RC. Is that also part of what drew you to pastel painting?

JK. Well, I think when I was at college I actually found it quite subversive. I liked the fact that I was doing pastels. At the time I think there was lots of macho painting going on. There was a kind of resurgence of huge, big, rather ugly paintings that really said "Oh, I'm here in the world". So I always felt like going more the opposite way. When we were younger,

my sister and I always thought that we'd end up in a small cottage together – it was like a dream – in long skirts, with our hair in buns, doing our paintings. I always had this romantic idea. I was always really happy when I was younger, on my own, in my bedroom, just doing my drawing. And I think that's still the same. I'm really happy. I mean I've got children around, but I'm still in my room doing my art, even though I'm older.

RC. I have this theory that artists are people who manage, one way or another, never to leave their childhood, never to have to go through disjuncture. It's not that you're immature: it's that you don't experience that discontinuity.

JK. There's no retirement age.

Rachel Cusk was born in 1967 and is the author of six novels: *Saving Agnes* (1993), which won the Whitbread First Novel Award; *The Temporary* (1995); *The Country Life* (1997), which won a Somerset Maugham Award; *The Lucky Ones* (2003), which was shortlisted for the Whitbread Novel Award; *In the Fold* (2005); and *Arlington Park* (2006), which was shortlisted for the 2007 Orange Broadband Prize for Fiction.

She has published two works of non-fiction: *A Life's Work: On Becoming a Mother* (2001) and *The Last Supper: A Summer in Italy* (2009). In 2003 she was chosen as one of Granta's Best of Young Novelists. She lives in Brighton.

Fence
Pastel on paper on board
2007
83 x 122 x 4cm

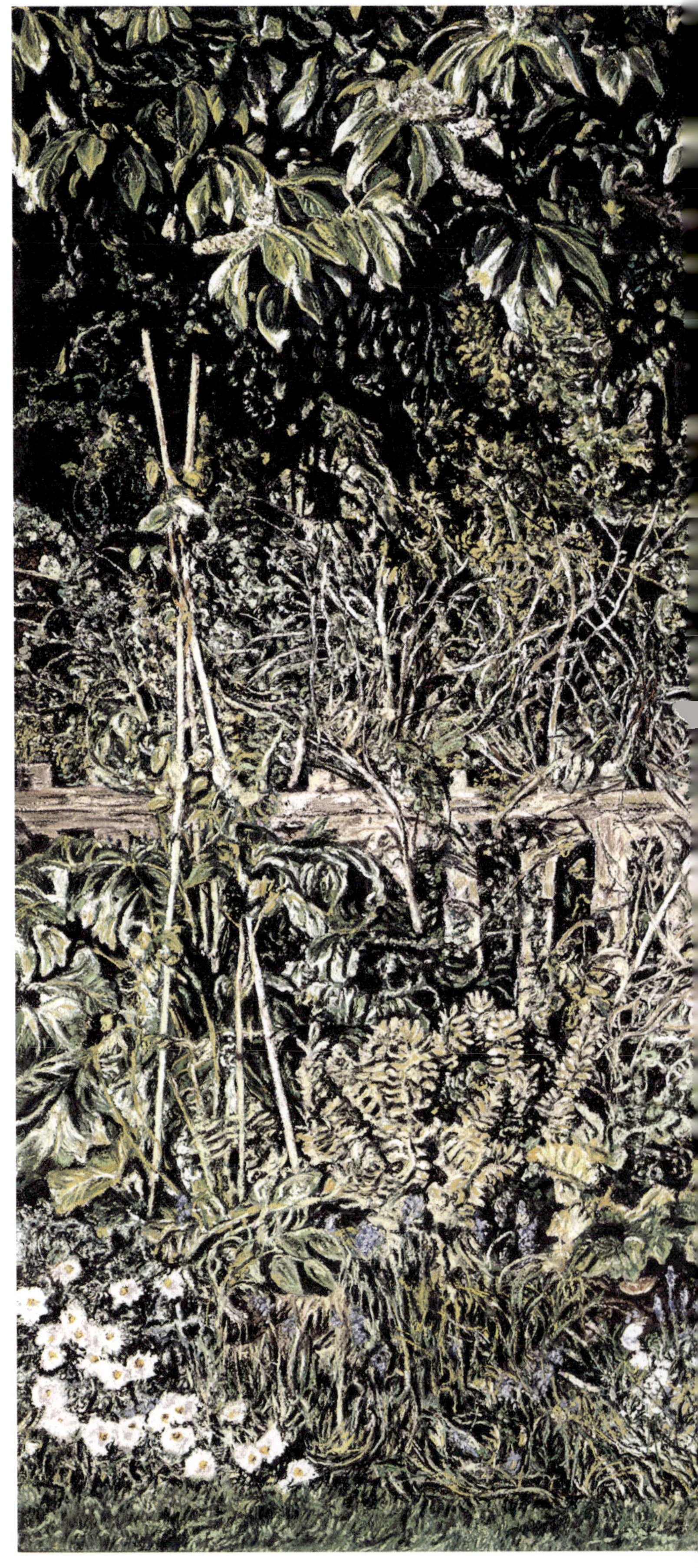

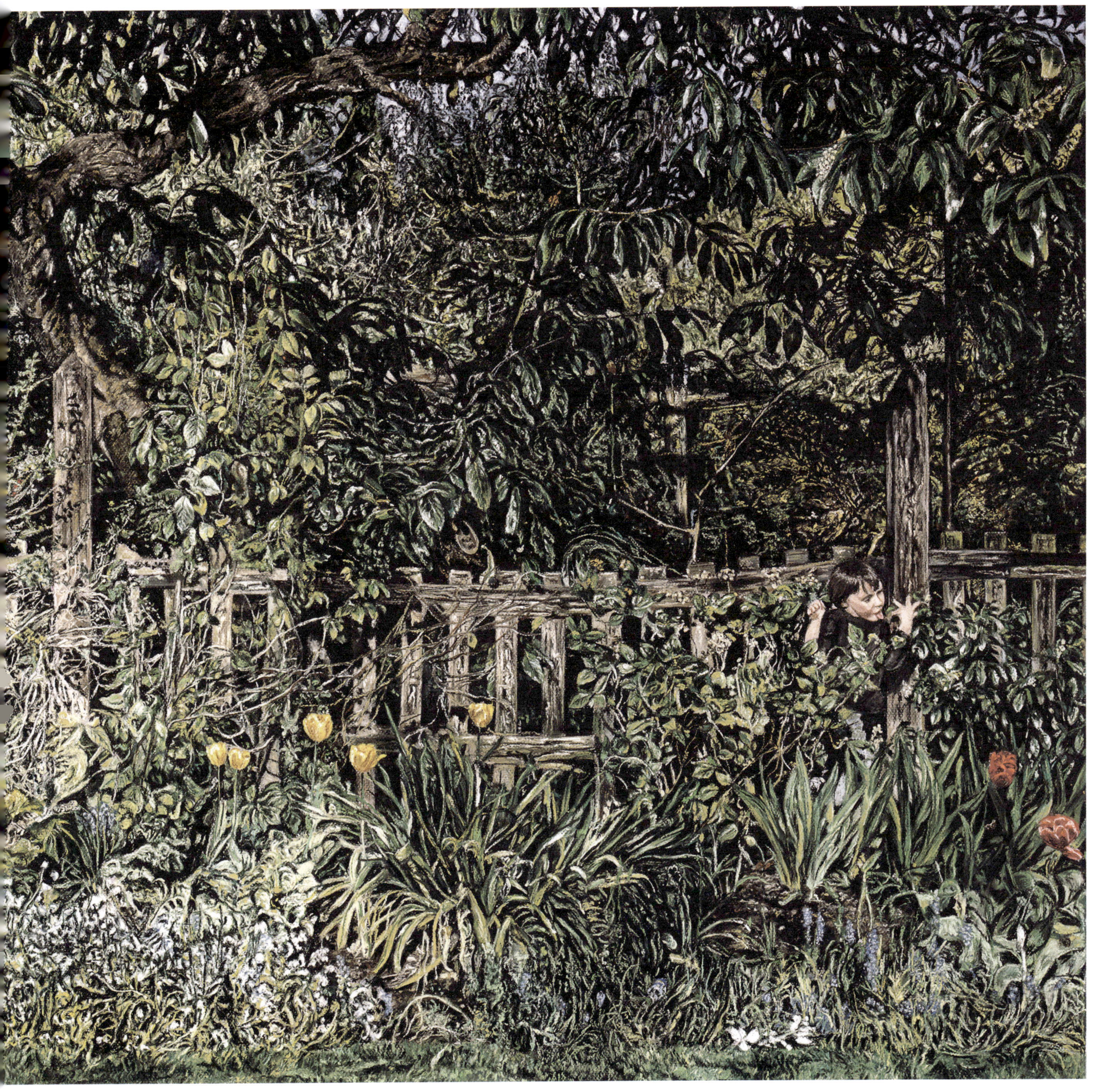

Leaves
Pastel on paper on board
2006
83 x 122 x 4cm

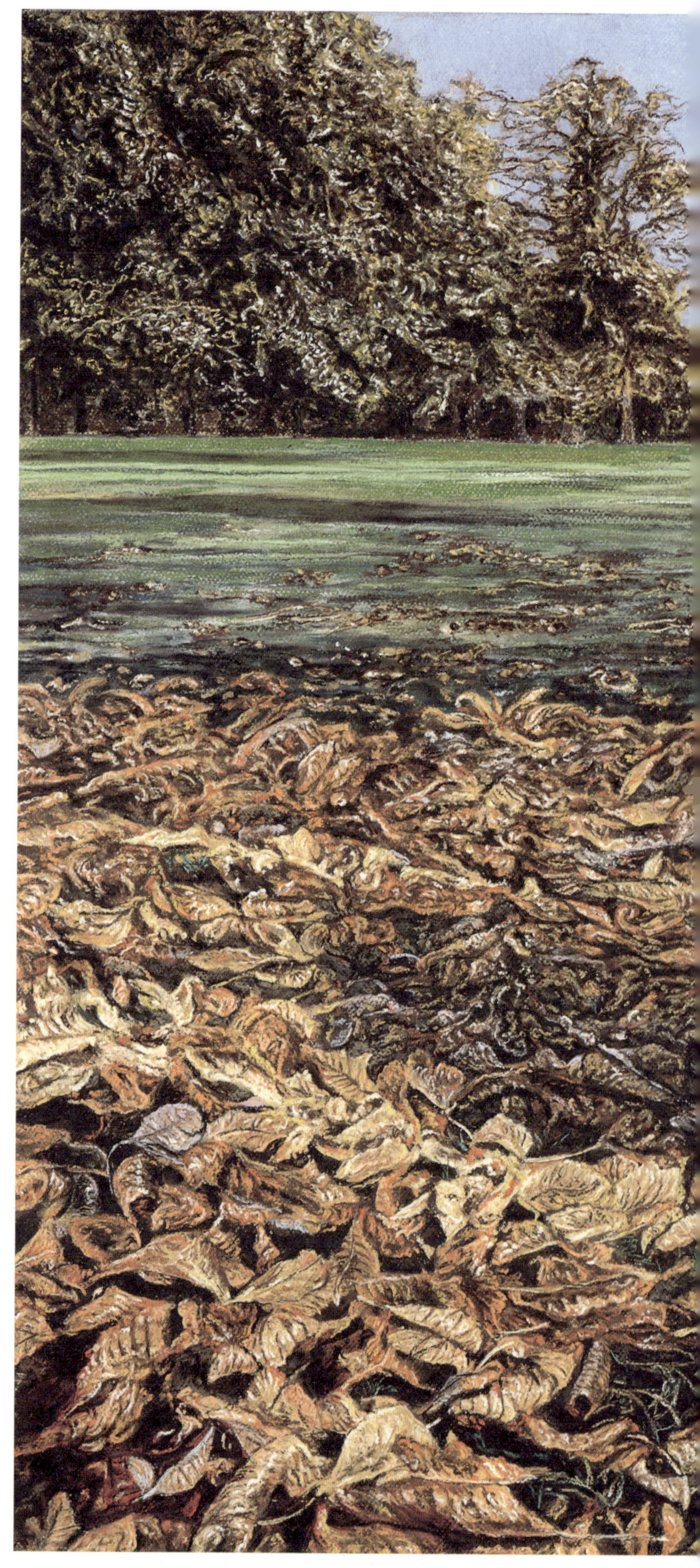

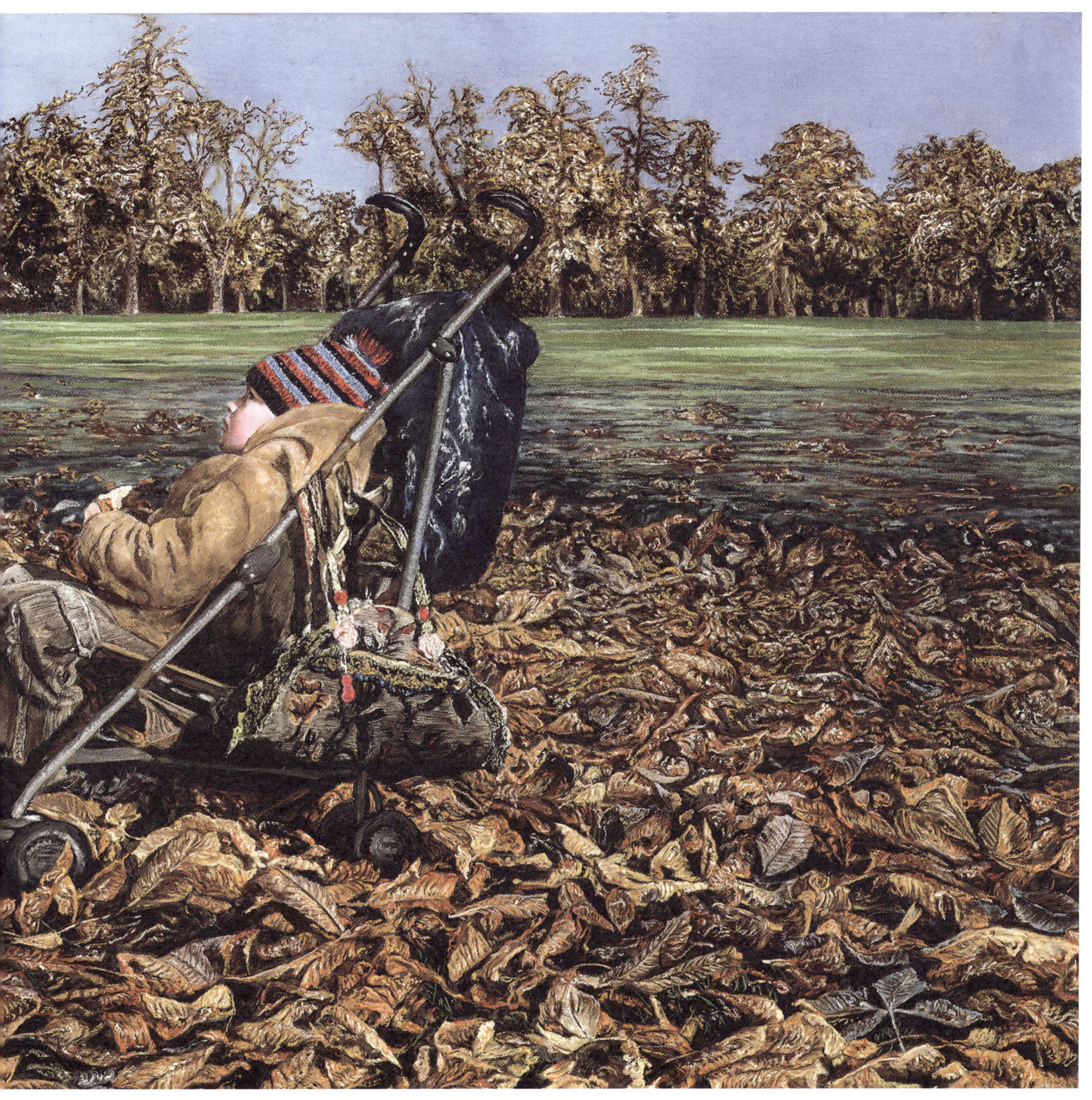

Rocks
Pastel on paper on board
2006
83 x 122 x 4cm

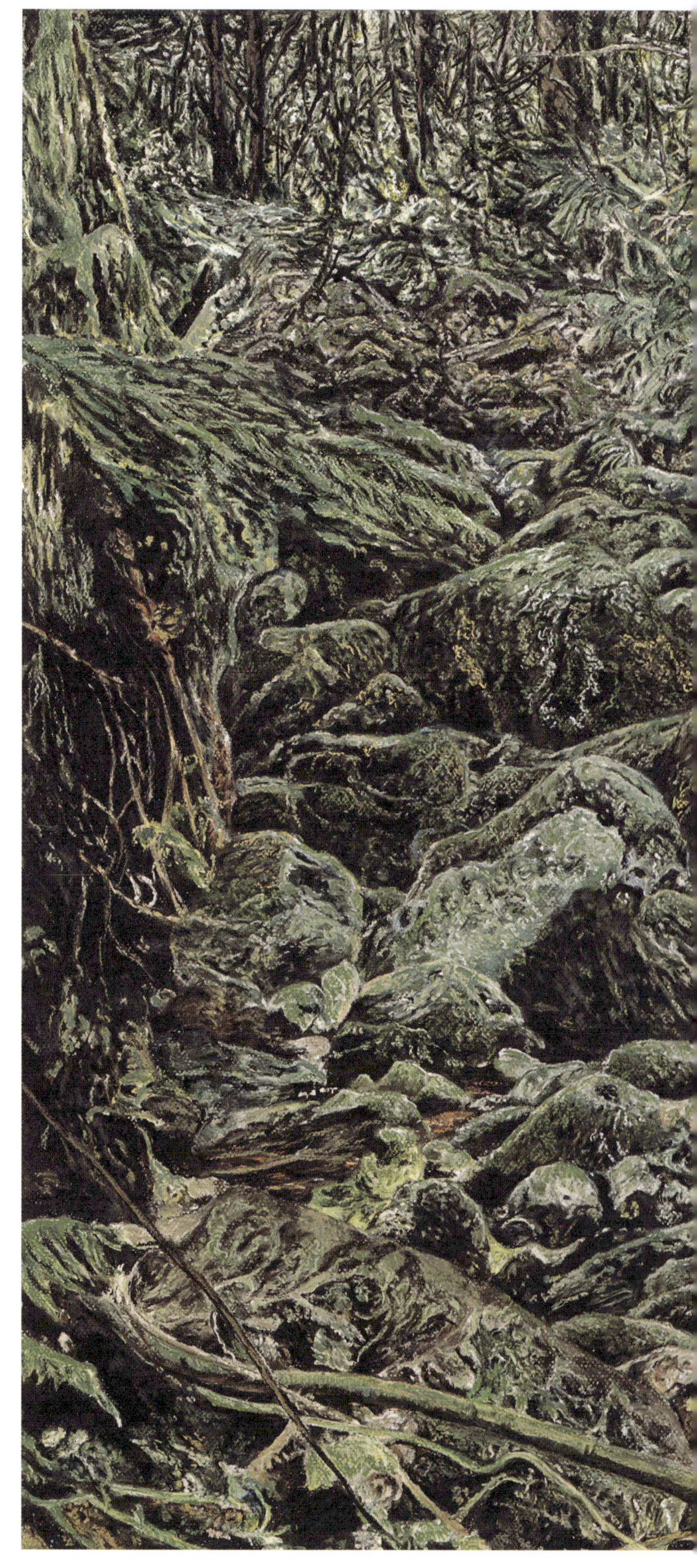

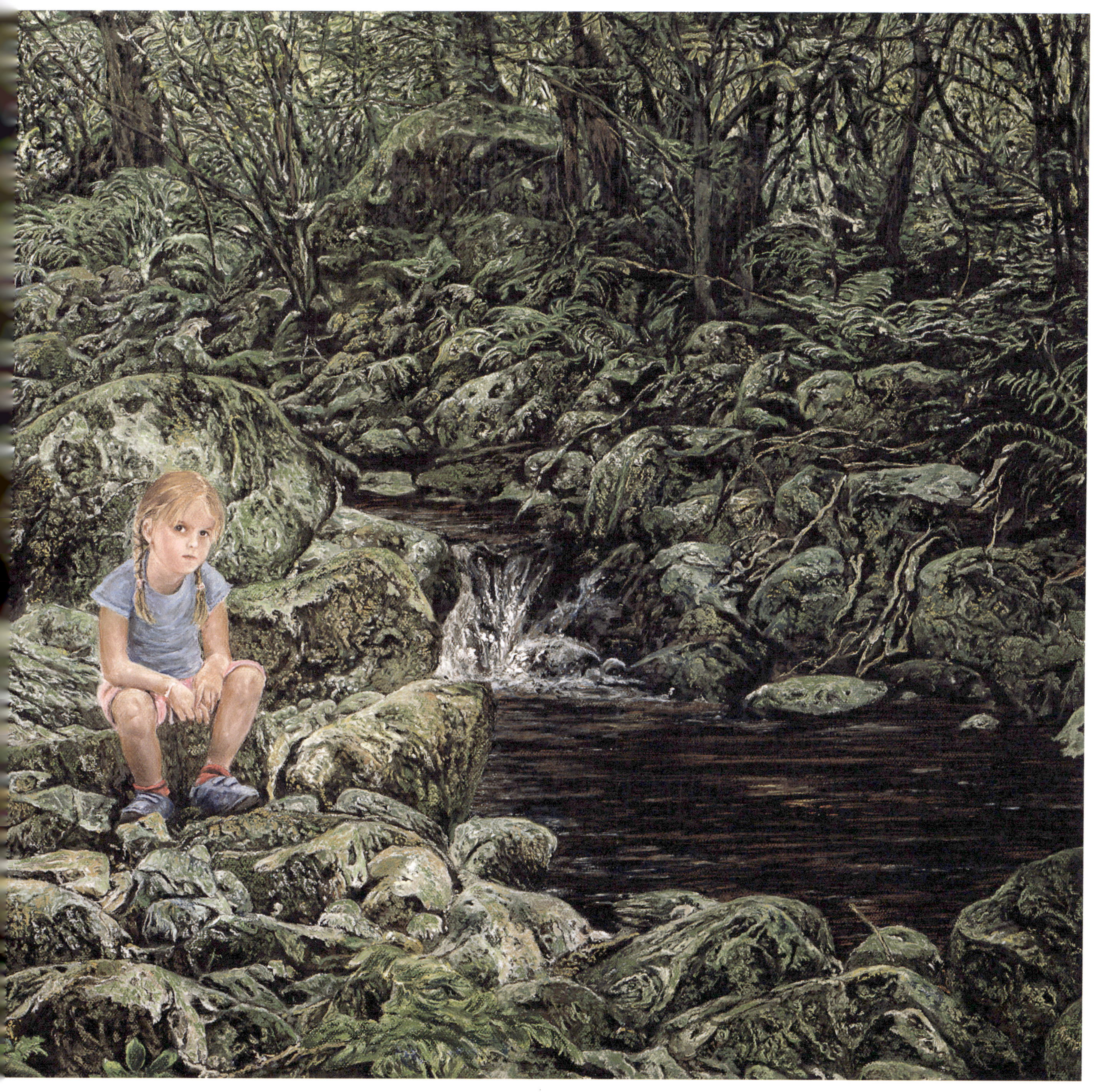

Roots
Pastel on paper on board
2007
83 x 122 x 4cm

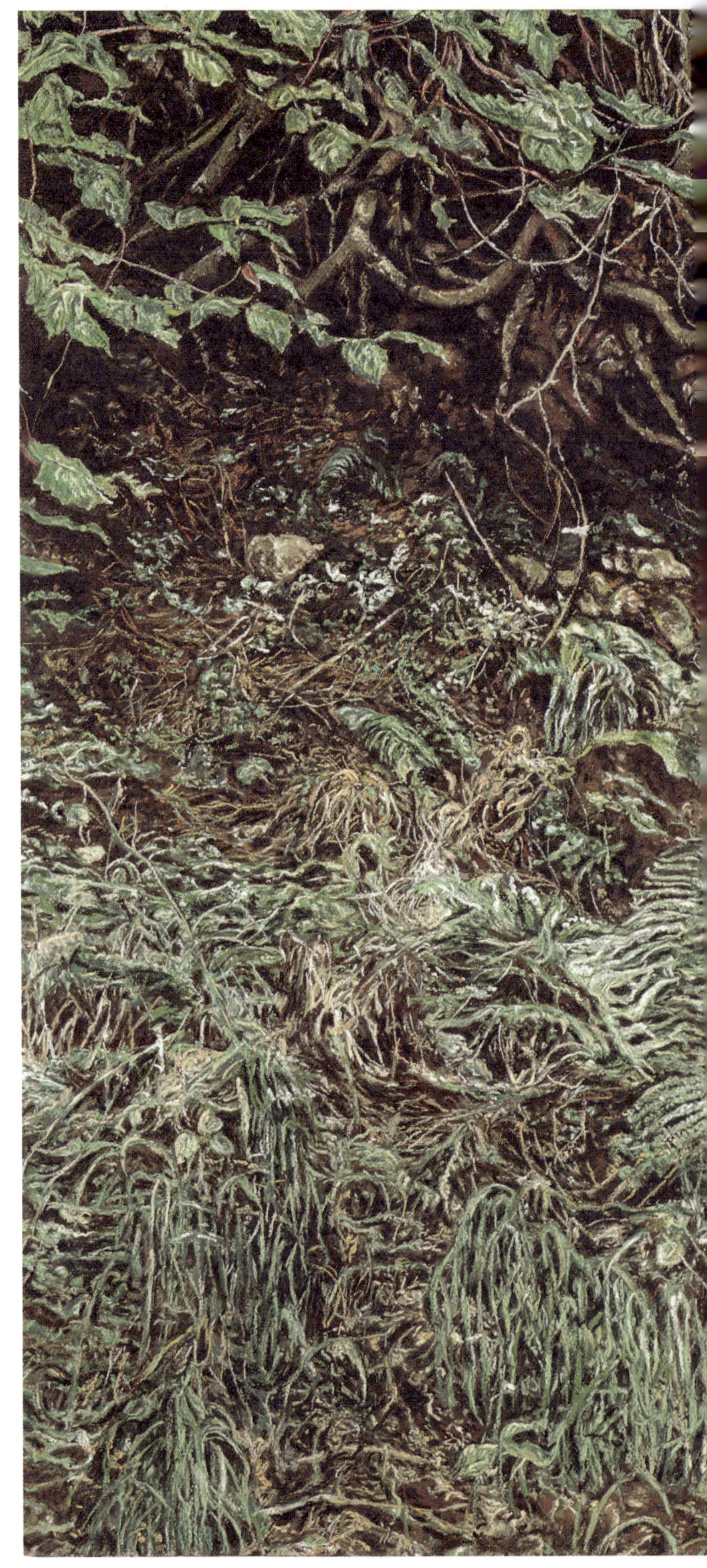

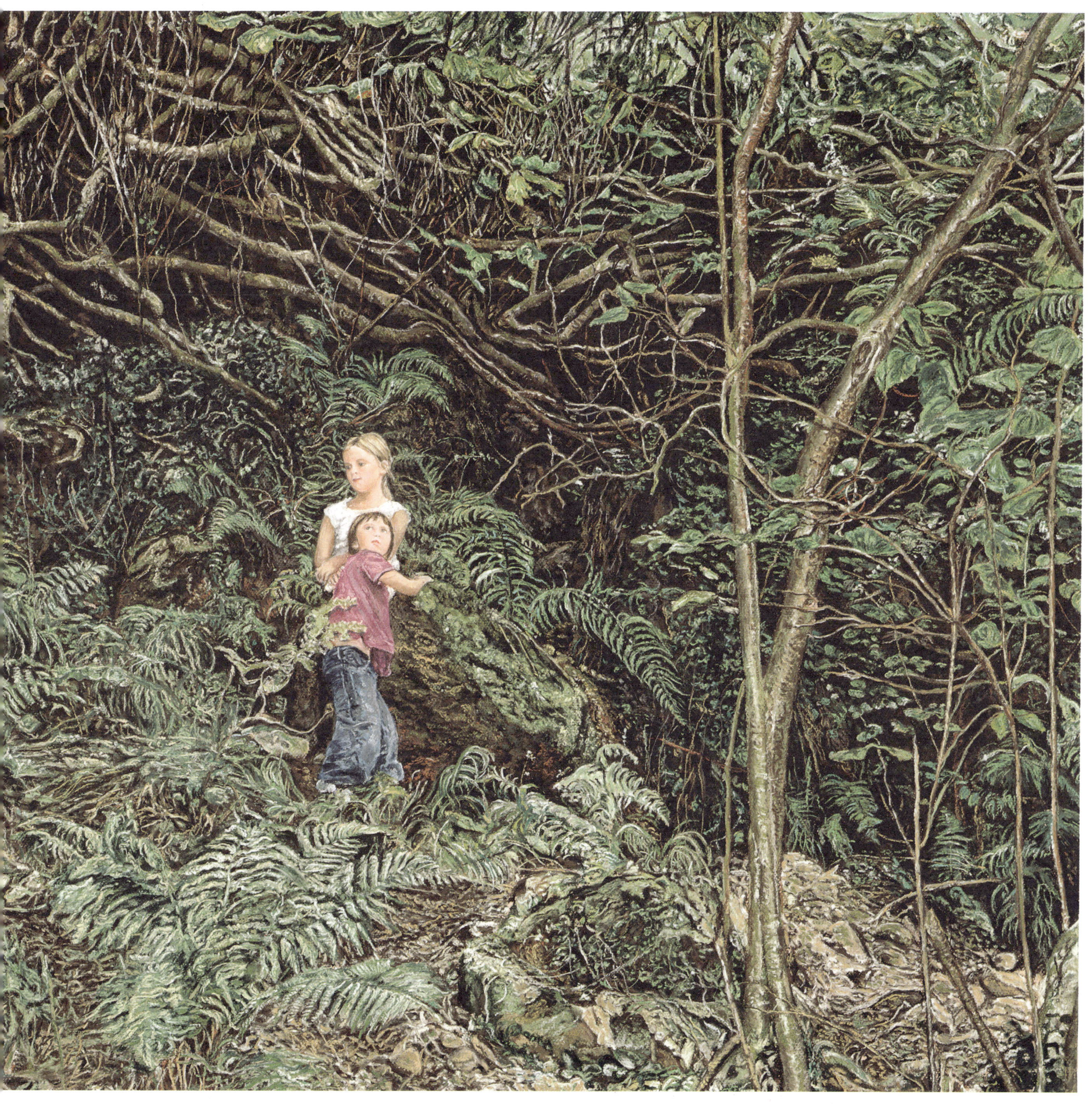

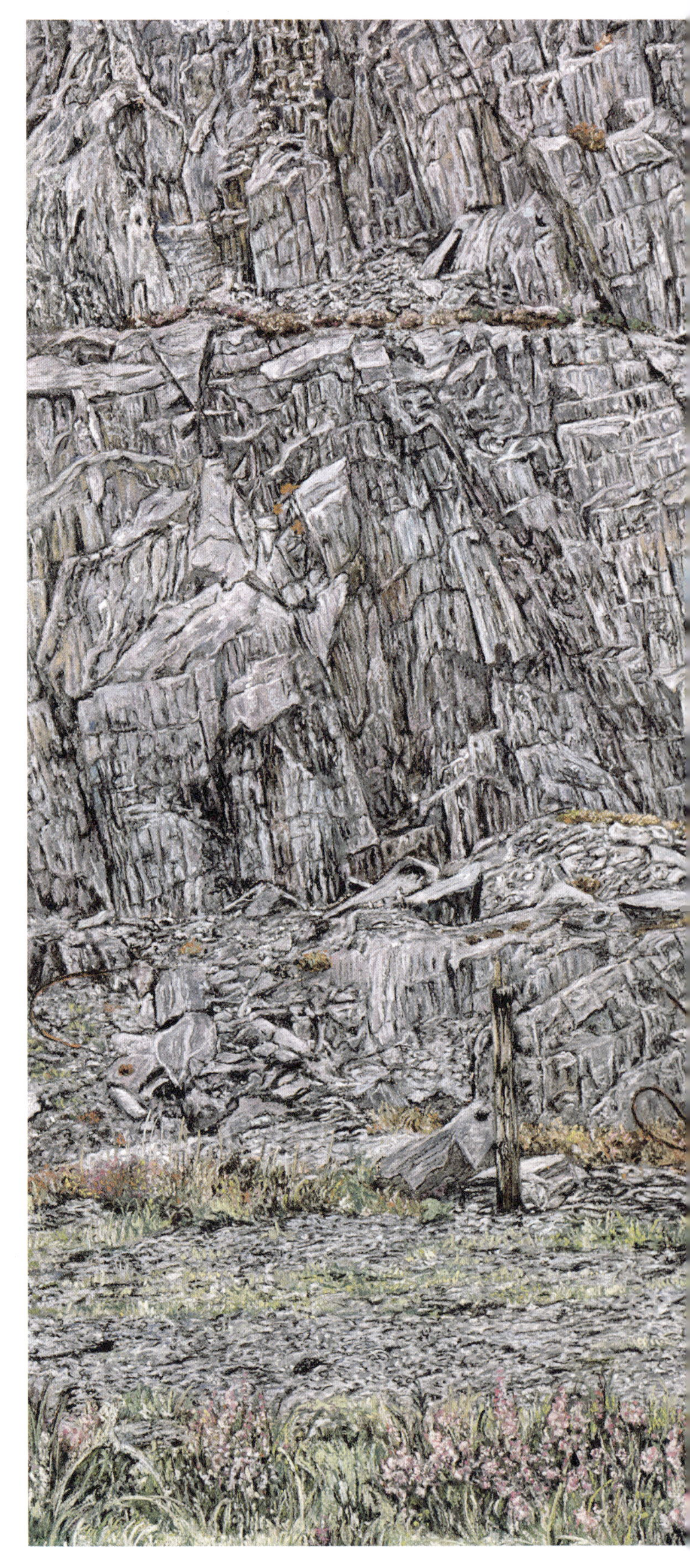

Slate
Pastel on paper on board
2008
83 x 122 x 4cm

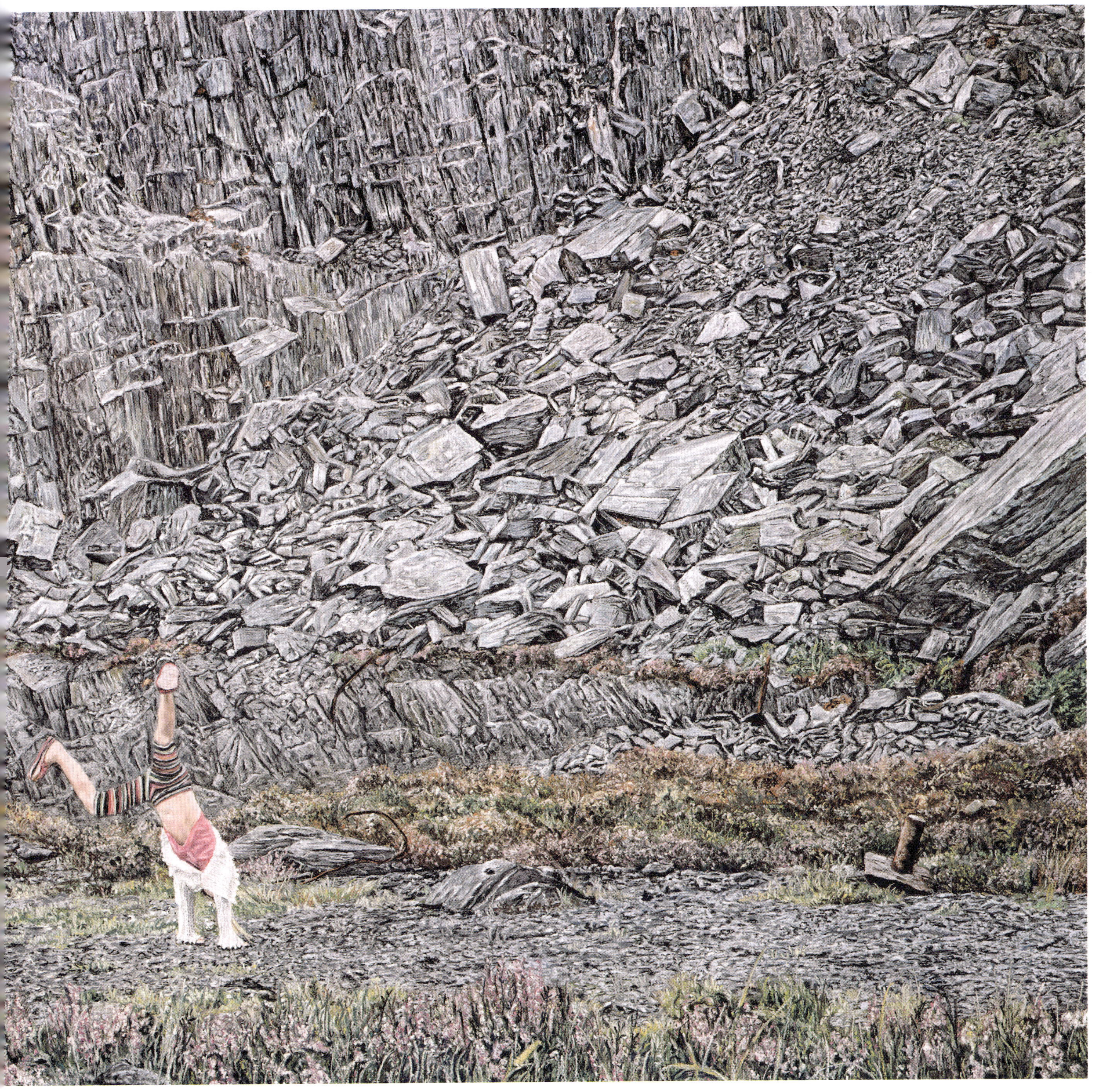

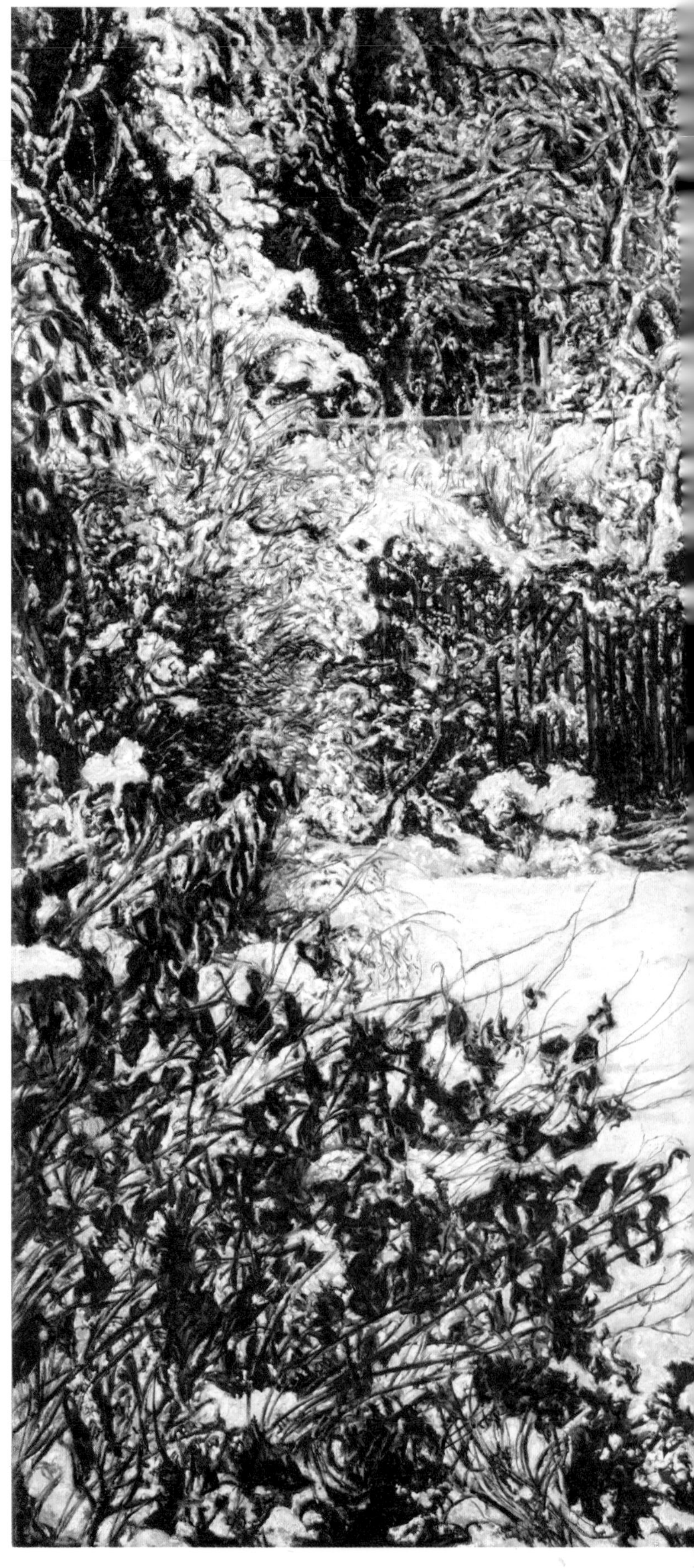

Snow
Pastel on paper on board
2005
83 x 122 x 4cm

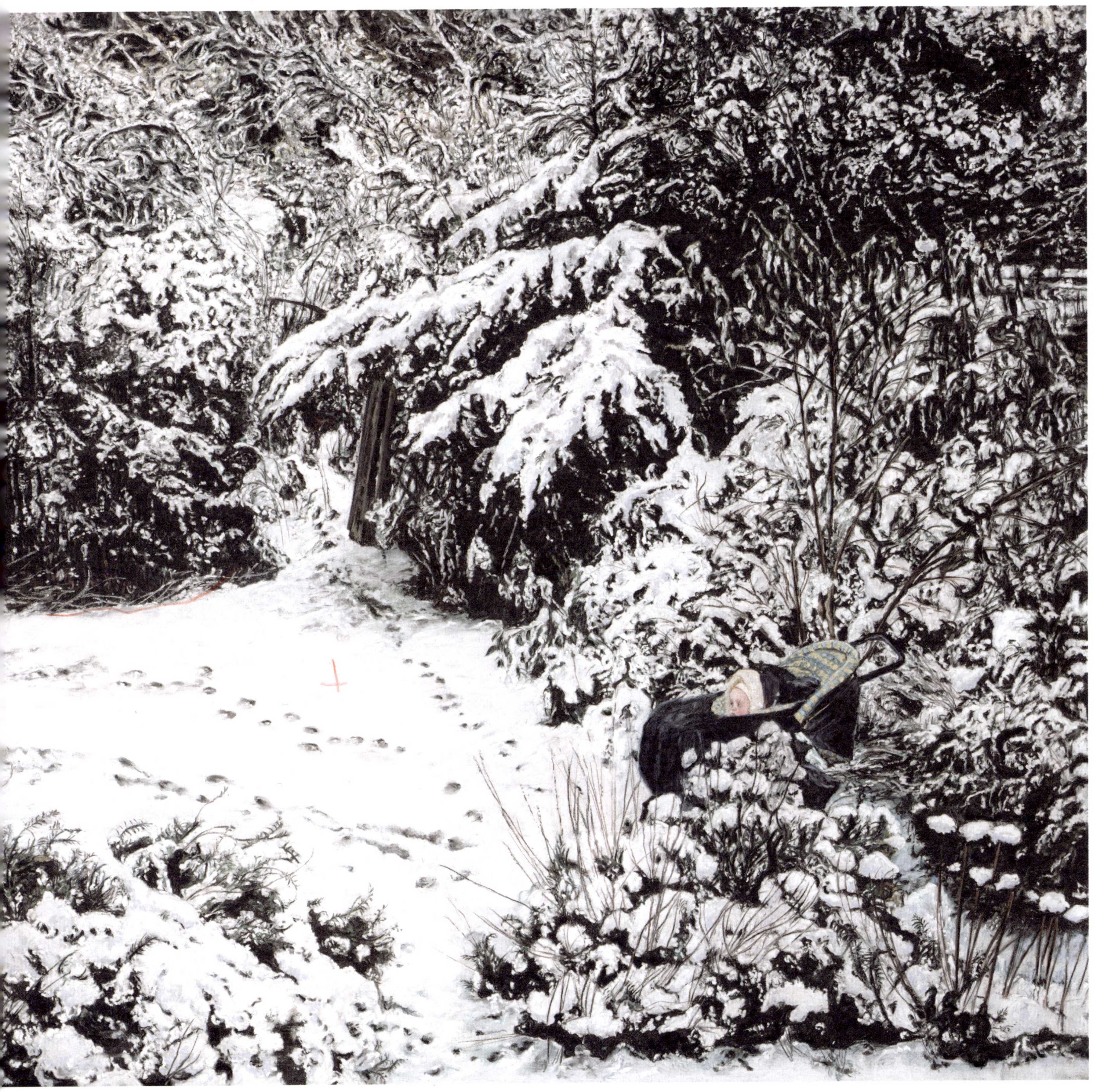

Wasteland
Pastel on paper on board
2006
83 x 122 x 4cm

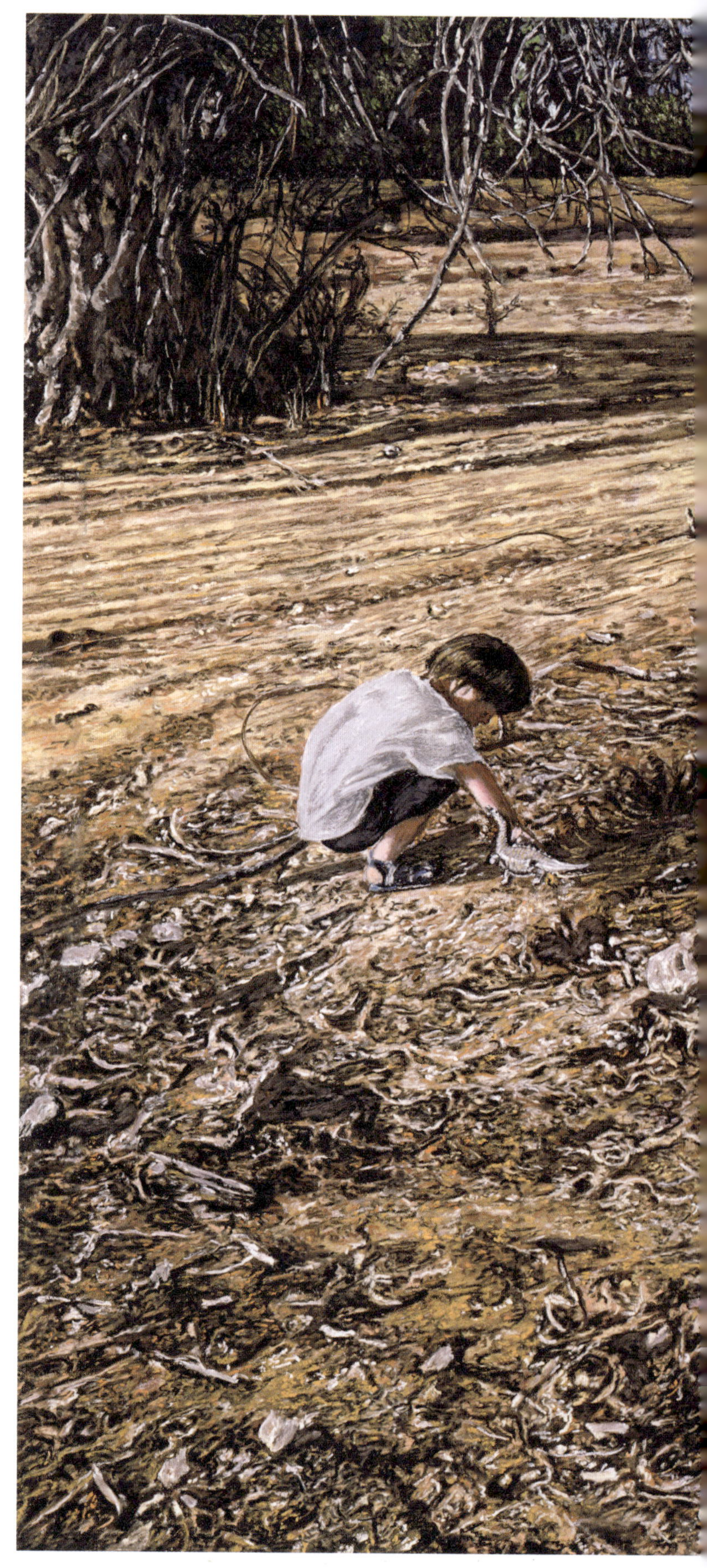

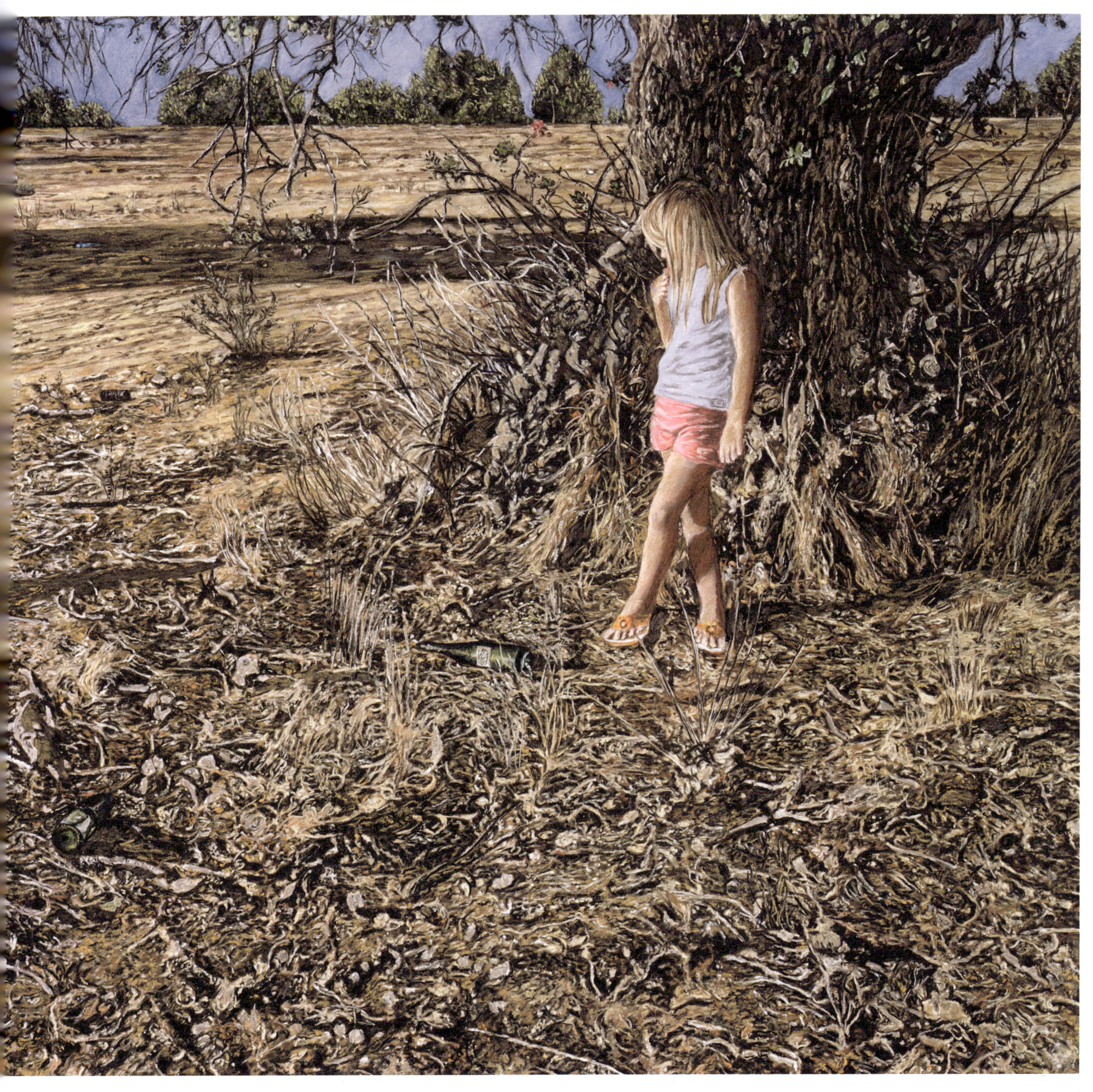

Wood
Pastel on paper on board
2008
83 x 122 x 4cm

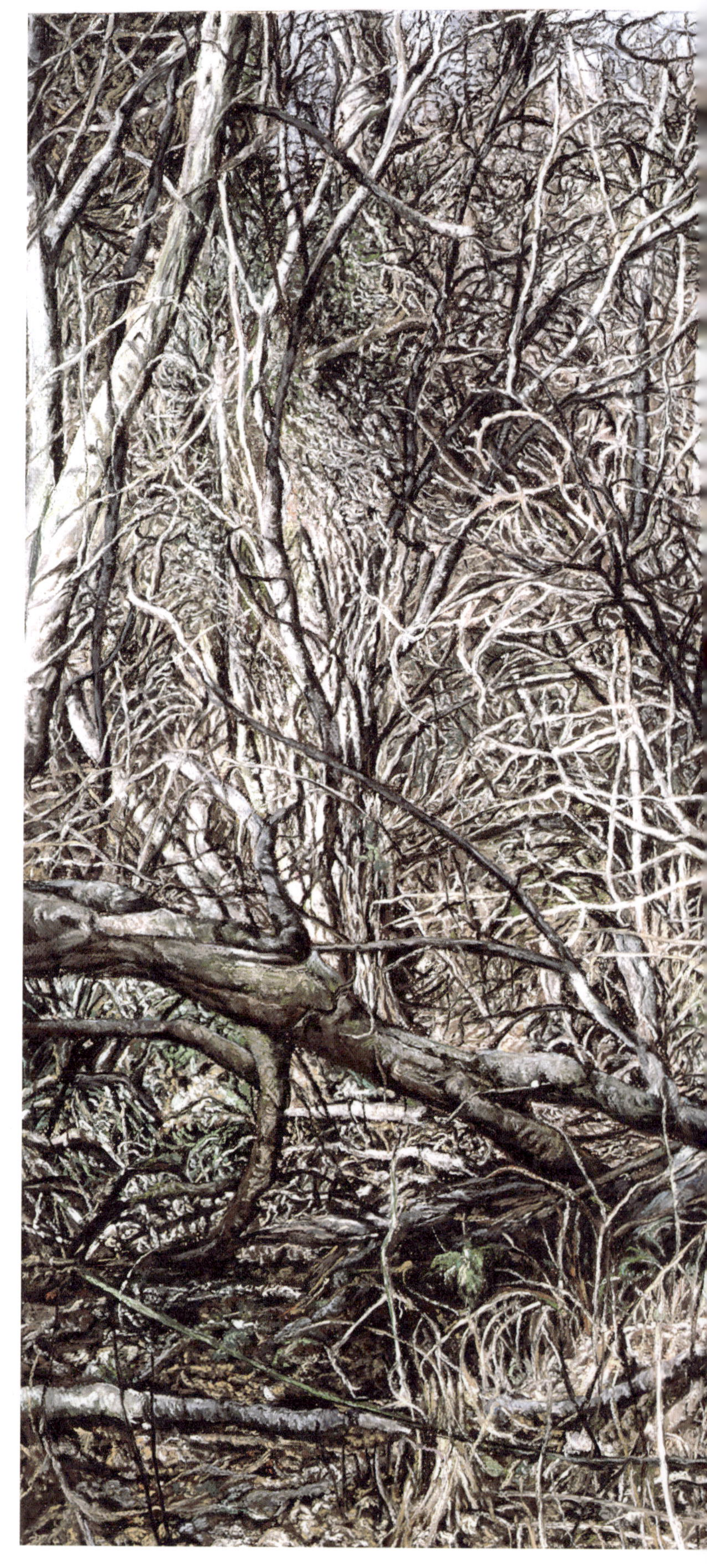

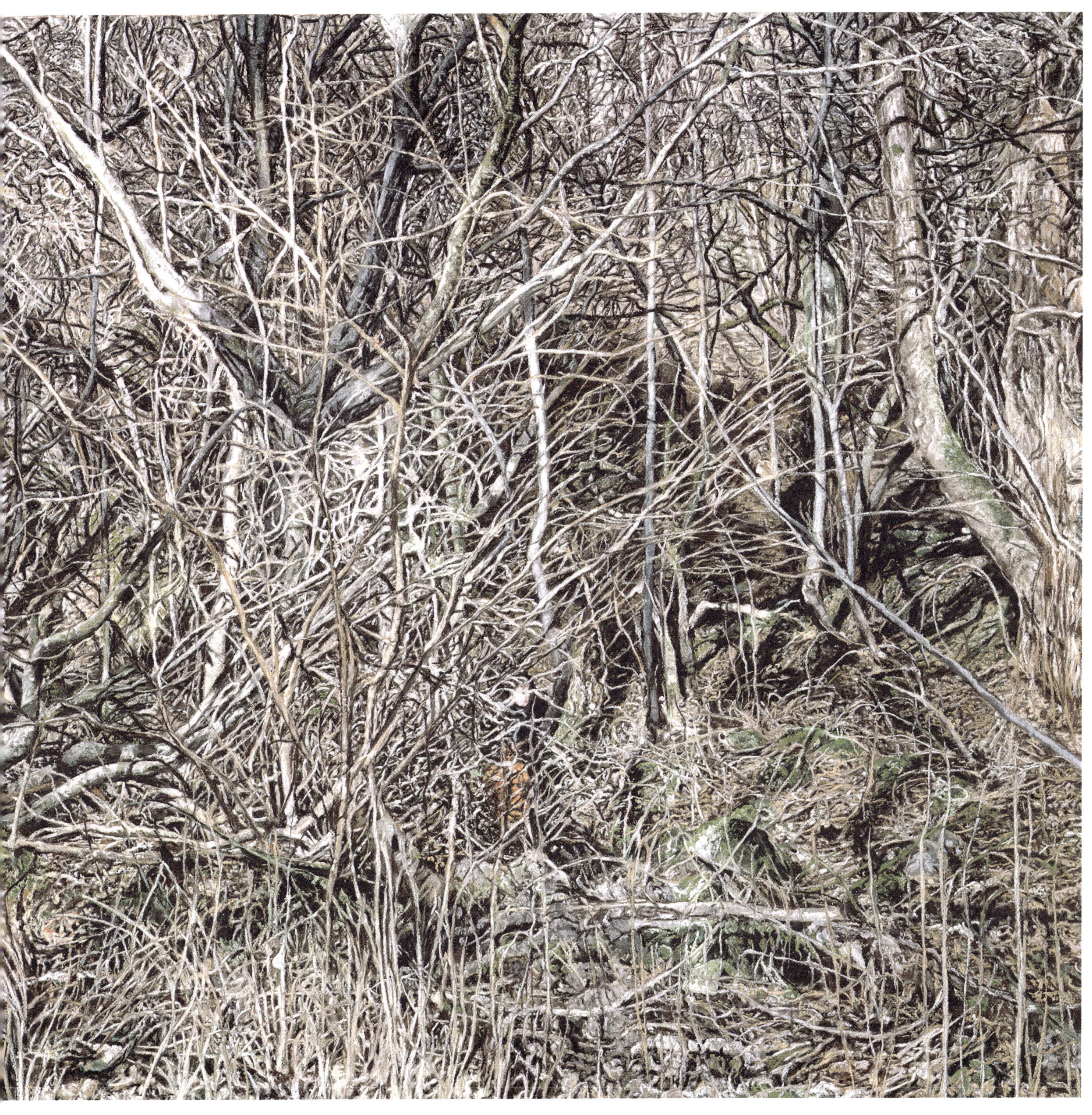

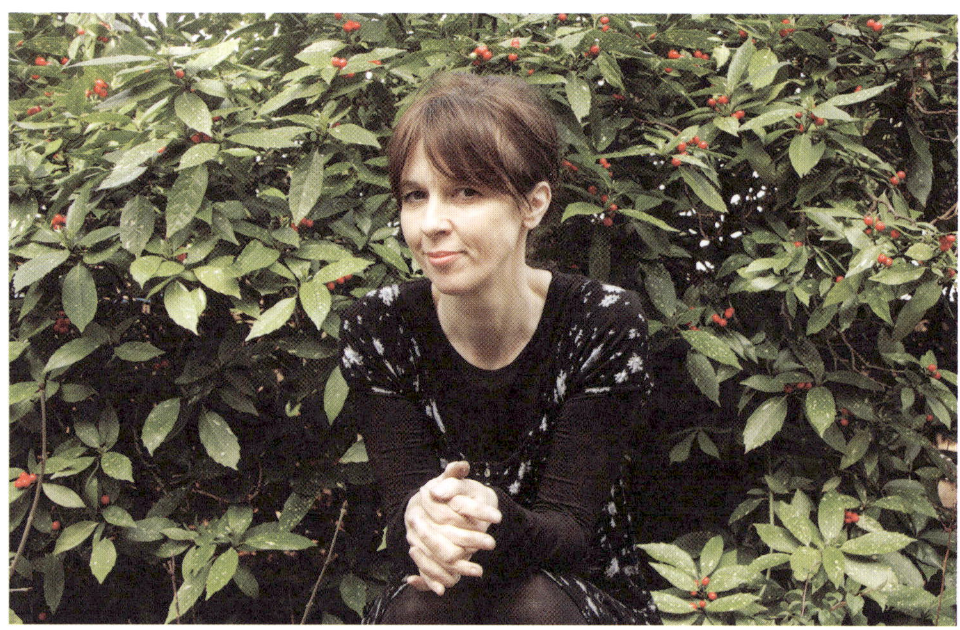

Joanna Kirk was born in Cheshire in 1963 and studied at Goldsmiths College, London. In 1988 she won the Whitechapel Gallery Artists Award and her work was exhibited at the touring 1990 British Art Show. She has participated in numerous exhibitions in Europe and the United States, including solo exhibitions in London, Glasgow, Milan, Bregenz, Cologne and Antwerp. She lives and works in Blackheath, London.